WHAT MAKES A

MONSTER?

Discovering the World's Scariest Creatures

by JESS KEATING

with illustrations by DAVID DeGRAND

Alfred A. Knopf
New York

What makes a MONSTER?

Turn the page
to find out,
if you dare....

Don't high-five the AYE-AYE.

Also known as the "demon primate," the AYE-AYE has a dangerous tool on hand. Or rather, its hand *is* a dangerous tool. With its witchlike claws, this lemur *tap, tap, taps* the trunks of trees, listening for changes in sound to find prey. Once it has found a tasty grub, the aye-aye uses its sharp teeth to gnaw into the bark, and with a yank, dinner is served.

TAP TAP TAP

The Stuff of Legends

The aye-aye is only dangerous if you're a bug, but many see it as a symbol of death. Some local Malagasy people believe the mere presence of an aye-aye can predict a villager's death. The Sakalava tribe also shares legends of aye-ayes sneaking into houses and using their long fingers to murder sleeping humans. Because of these superstitions, aye-ayes are often killed on sight. Today, they are listed as endangered.

Name: Aye-aye

Species name: *Daubentonia madagascariensis*

Size: Roughly 15.7 inches (39.9 centimeters), with another 22–24 inches (55.9–61 centimeters) of tail

Diet: Insects and insect larvae found under tree bark, as well as seeds

Habitat: The forests of Madagascar

Predators and threats: The fossa (a catlike mammal), domestic dogs, and snakes will all eat aye-ayes. Humans are the aye-ayes biggest threats, as their natural habitat is often cleared for agriculture. Local superstitions are also to blame for decreasing aye-aye numbers.

Don't dine with the VAMPIRE BAT.

Stealthy **VAMPIRE BATS** wait for the cover of darkness to feed, preying on cows, horses, or even humans. Using special heat sensors in their noses, the bats can tell where warm blood is close to the skin. Then they use their sharp teeth to bite. Unlike Dracula, they don't actually suck blood. Instead, they lap it up like a cat.

Sharing Is Scaring!

Vampire bats may drink blood, but they're also generous creatures. Living in **colonies** of a hundred or more, these bats are like one big, batty family. If a bat in a colony can't find a meal, other bats may **regurgitate** their own to share with it. It sounds gross, but is it any different than sharing your sandwich at school?

Name: Vampire bat

Species name: *Desmodus rotundus*

Size: 3.5 inches (8.9 centimeters) from head to tail, with a wingspan of 7 inches (17.8 centimeters)

Diet: As juveniles, vampire bats drink milk. As adults, they feed on blood.

Habitat: The tropical and subtropical regions of Mexico, Central America, and South America

Predators and threats: Active at night, vampire bats must watch out for eagles, hawks, and snakes. Many humans also hunt these bats, to prevent them from biting their livestock.

Don't badger the HONEY BADGER.

Armed with strong jaws, sharp teeth, and a nasty personality, **HONEY BADGERS** are known as the world's most fearless creatures in the *Guinness Book of World Records*. They pick fights with leopards, lions, hyenas, and even porcupines. Their thick, rubbery skin is tough enough to withstand arrows and spears, and so loose they can easily squirm free from a predator's grasp.

Sleep It Off!

Honey badgers often eat venomous snakes like puff adders, but how do the badgers avoid getting bitten? The answer: they don't. Scientists aren't yet certain how honey badgers survive deadly snakebites, but they can resist the effects of most venoms. When they are bitten, honey badgers seem to fall asleep, then wake up a few hours later as if nothing has happened. There's a nap you'd never forget!

YAWN!

? CHOMP!

Name: Honey badger

Species name: *Mellivora capensis*

Size: 36–39 inches (91.4–99.1 centimeters) from head to tail, 9–12 inches (22.9–30.5 centimeters) at the shoulder

Diet: Almost everything! Badgers love honey (it's how they got their name), but they will also eat insects, beetles, scorpions, birds, rodents, snakes, tortoises, carrion, and fruit.

Habitat: Grasslands and dry forests of Africa (from southern Morocco to the southern tip of Africa) and Asia, including Turkmenistan, Nepal, Afghanistan, and western India

Predators and threats: Frequently targeted by beekeepers and livestock farmers, honey badgers are also killed for their pelts and used in traditional medicines. Few animals prey on honey badgers due to their aggressive nature.

Never poke the PORTUGUESE MAN-OF-WAR.

Surprise! The **PORTUGUESE MAN-OF-WAR** isn't just one animal—it's a *group* of animals all acting as one. Many specialized organisms called **zooids** join together to form its body. Some zooids are in charge of digestion or reproduction, while others form the tentacles that sway beneath the water. These tentacles are loaded with venom-filled **nematocysts**, ready to fire like poisoned harpoons into unlucky prey.

Hey, Sailor!
The man-of-war gets its name from the large gas-filled float that is visible on the water, much like an old warship at sail. It might seem like it's at the mercy of the ocean current, but the man-of-war can direct its course by raising or lowering this sail, just like a real ship.

Name: Portuguese man-of-war

Species name: *Physalia physalis*

Size: Float: 1 foot (30 centimeters) long and 5 inches (12.7 centimeters) wide, with tentacles typically 30 feet (9.1 meters) long, though they can reach up to 165 feet (50.3 meters) long!

Diet: Small fish, plankton, and other ocean animals

Habitat: The tropical and subtropical waters of the world's oceans; they have also been spotted in the waters near Long Island and the Jersey Shore!

Predators and threats: Nudibranchs, sand crabs, and sea turtles all feed on man-of-wars. Global climate change is throwing off the balance of marine ecosystems, yet more research is needed to determine how this affects man-of-war populations.

Never shake hands with the HORROR FROG.

Boasting one of the creepiest abilities in the animal kingdom, the **HORROR FROG** isn't your ordinary **amphibian.** When it is threatened, this frog breaks the bones inside its own hand, creating sharp "bone claws" that shoot out through its skin. Intense! Not surprisingly, this frog is also sometimes known as the Wolverine frog.

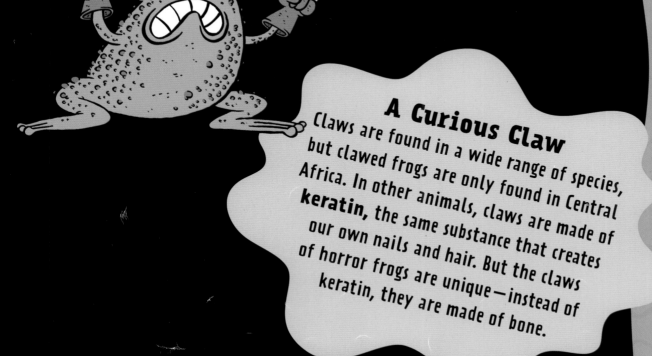

A Curious Claw

Claws are found in a wide range of species, but clawed frogs are only found in Central Africa. In other animals, claws are made of **keratin**, the same substance that creates our own nails and hair. But the claws of horror frogs are unique—instead of keratin, they are made of bone.

Name: Horror frog (also called the hairy frog or Wolverine frog)

Species name: *Trichobatrachus robustus*

Size: 4.3 inches (10.9 centimeters) from nose to rear

Diet: Spiders, beetles, grasshoppers, slugs, millipedes, and centipedes

Habitat: The subtropical and tropical forests, rivers, plantations, and lowlands of Nigeria, Cameroon, Democratic Republic of the Congo, Equatorial Guinea, and Gabon

Predators and threats: Along with animal predators such as monkeys and birds of prey, the horror frog is also hunted by some humans for food. Like many animals, it is threatened by habitat loss.

Hide from the GREATER HONEYGUIDE.

HONEYGUIDES are named for their love of honey, but their behavior is less than sweet. Adult honeyguides don't take care of their own babies. Instead, they lay their eggs in the nests of other bird species. When a honeyguide chick hatches, it uses its sharp, hooked beak to attack its foster siblings, often killing them. What better way to eliminate the competition for food?

Brutal Birds

Animals that trick others into caring for their young are called **brood parasites**. But honeyguide parents don't just dupe other birds into raising their young for them. Sometimes they will even peck and destroy eggs that other honeyguides have laid in the same foster nest, to ensure *their* soon-to-hatch chick gets the best crack at survival.

Name: Greater honeyguide

Species name: *Indicator indicator*

Size: Roughly 7.9 inches (20 centimeters) long

Diet: Bee eggs, larvae, and pupae; beeswax; some flying insects; and termites. Honeyguides are also known to eat the eggs of other small birds.

Habitat: The open woods, woodlands, bushlands, plantations, and thickets of sub-Saharan Africa

Predators and threats: There are no known animal predators of the honeyguide, and their numbers have increased due to man-made woodland habitats.

Steer clear of the CORDYCEPS FUNGUS.

Sometimes the biggest monsters aren't animals at all. When the **CORDYCEPS FUNGUS** (also called the zombie ant fungus) infects an insect, it takes over its brain and forces it to crawl to the end of a branch. Once there, the insect dies, and the fungus bursts through its head, ready to grow new **spores** to infect other insects.

A Helpful Zombie?

Fungi like cordyceps might seem like monsters, but nature works in peculiar ways. Cordyceps are actually good for **biodiversity**. There are thousands of species of cordyceps, and each targets a different species living in the jungle. Ecosystems need balance, and **parasites** like cordyceps ensure that the population of no single species grows too large. This gives everyone a chance to survive. It's not pretty, but it works!

All hail, Fungus!

Name: Cordyceps

Species name: *Ophiocordyceps unilateralis*

Size: Cordyceps spores are extremely tiny (roughly 20–100 micrometers).

Diet: Cordyceps parasitize insects and other arthropods, each species targeting a specific host.

Habitat: The tropical forests of Thailand, Central America, and Africa and the rain forests of Brazil. The caterpillar fungus species (*Ophiocordyceps sinensis*) is found throughout Asia.

Predators and threats: Cordyceps have been used as traditional medicine in some areas of Tibet and China. There are no known animal predators.

Check your shoe for the DEATHSTALKER SCORPION.

Armed with predatory **pincers** and a stinging tail, the **DEATHSTALKER** is one of the deadliest scorpions in the world, and its tiny, flat body makes it easy to hide in crevices or under rocks. People often mistake it for a plastic toy, but this is one animal you don't want to play with!

Dr. Deathstalker, at Your Service!

Deathstalker venom can be harmful—even lethal!—but doctors have discovered that it can also be used to treat people with brain cancer. Usually, it is very difficult to tell **tumor cells** from healthy cells. But components of deathstalker venom are able to "paint" cancerous cells, so doctors can easily spot them. This allows doctors to safely remove the cancerous cells without affecting healthy ones. Someday deathstalkers might need a new name for all the lives they save!

Name: Deathstalker scorpion

Species name: *Leiurus quinquestriatus*

Size: 1.2–3 inches long (3–7.6 centimeters)

Diet: Crickets and other small insects

Habitat: Dry, rocky desert and scrubland regions of the Middle East and North Africa

Predators and threats: Despite their stinging tails, deathstalkers are preyed upon by rodents, lizards, snakes, birds, and bats. Humans also pose a threat to scorpions, often squishing them if they are found near human homes.

Beware the PRAIRIE DOG.

What's so scary about a sweet little **PRAIRIE DOG**? Prairie dog fleas can carry the deadly **bubonic plague.** This is the same disease that killed an estimated 50 million people in the Middle Ages. Infected fleas can jump from prairie dogs to domestic pets, so it's very important to de-flea your cats and dogs!

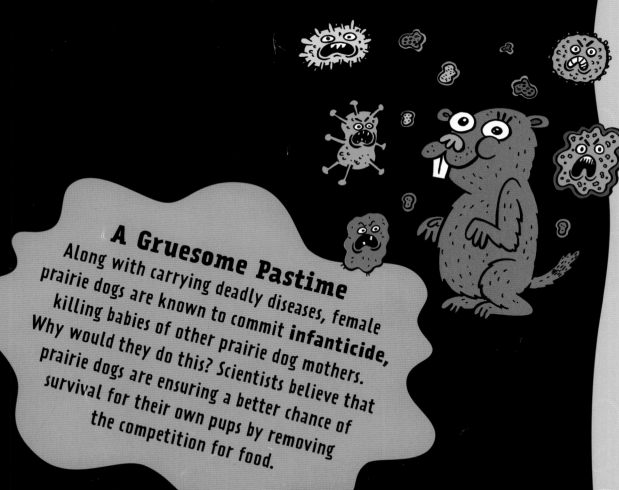

A Gruesome Pastime

Along with carrying deadly diseases, female prairie dogs are known to commit **infanticide,** killing babies of other prairie dog mothers. Why would they do this? Scientists believe that prairie dogs are ensuring a better chance of survival for their own pups by removing the competition for food.

Name: Black-tailed prairie dog

Species name: *Cynomys ludovicianus*

Size: Approximately 12–17 inches (30.5–43.2 centimeters), with a 3-to-4-inch (7.6-to-10.2-centimeter) tail

Diet: Seeds, grasses, roots, buds, and fruits, along with insects, such as caterpillars and grasshoppers

Habitat: The grassland, shortgrass and mixed-grass prairies, desert grassland, and sagebrush steppes of North America

Predators and threats: Prairie dogs are common prey for coyotes, foxes, badgers, birds of prey, rattlesnakes, and bobcats. Loss of habitat and increased human development all affect the prairie dog population.

Don't play dress-up with the ASSASSIN BUG.

What's black and orange and *dead* all over? The ASSASSIN BUG has monstrous taste in clothes. Like many other insects, this bug eats ants. But instead of discarding the **exoskeletons** of its victims, the assassin bug uses a sticky substance to glue them onto its back. It can wear up to twenty ant corpses at a time! Talk about a fashion statement.

Dressed to Kill

What's the point of getting dressed up in the bodies of your victims? Not only do the ant bodies provide a sturdy set of armor, but they can also confuse prey by masking the assassin bugs' natural smell. The bodies might also protect them from predators. Jumping spiders often hunt assassin bugs, but they avoid bugs in armor.

Name: Assas~~

**Species nam~~
petax

Size: Roughly 0.4 inc~~ (1 centimeter) in length

Diet: Ants

Habitat: The forests of East Africa and Malaysia

Predators and threats: Assassin bugs have many enemies, including birds, rodents, praying mantises, spiders, and other assassin bugs.

Be wary of the FANGTOOTH MORAY EEL.

Not only do **FANGTOOTH MORAY EELS** look monstrous, they have a reputation for lashing out at scuba divers, and even biting off the fingers of those who try to feed them! But don't judge them too quickly—these morays are acting out of self-defense, protecting their homes. Like many "monsters," the fangtooth moray eel doesn't attack unless provoked.

That's a Moray!

There are about two hundred different species of moray eel, but they all have impressive jaws—two sets of them! Moray eels have a *second* set of jaws in the back of their throats. These **pharyngeal jaws** extend forward, grasping prey from the moray's front teeth and dragging it back into its throat. This unusual **adaptation** might seem freaky, but you have little to fear unless you're a fish!

Name: Fangtooth moray eel

Species name: *Enchelycore anatina*

Size: 43–47 inches (109.2–119.4 centimeters) long

Diet: Fish, crustaceans, shrimp, and mollusks

Habitat: The warm waters of the eastern Atlantic Ocean, including the Mediterranean Sea, Madeira, Cape Verde, the Azores, and the Canary Islands

Predators and threats: Moray eels have few predators besides barracudas, sharks, and sea snakes.

Keep your eye on the TYRANT LEECH KING.

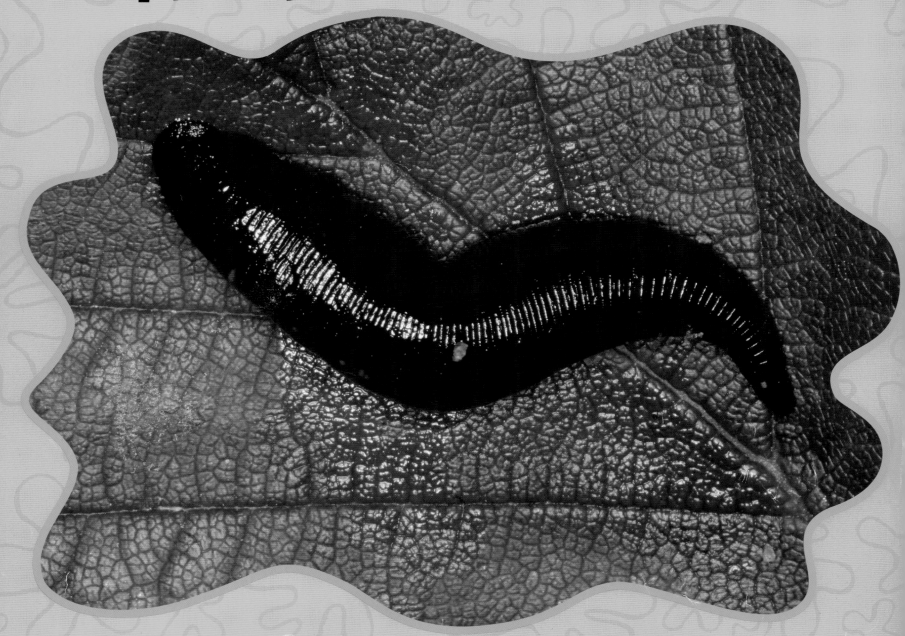

The **TYRANT LEECH KING** has one jaw with eight teeth that it uses to saw into the flesh of other animals. Unlike some other leeches, the tyrant leech king doesn't just attach to its host from the outside. This monster hides *inside* its host, in a nostril or other orifice. Once there, this leech can spend days or even weeks drinking blood.

Leech Mania!

Despite how creepy they are, leeches have been used in medicine for centuries. Doctors used to apply living leeches to patients' skin, in a process called **bloodletting.** It was thought that bloodletting could prevent and treat diseases. Today, we know that's not true, but doctors still sometimes use medicinal leeches to help the **circulation** of people healing from surgery!

Name: Tyrant leech king

Species name: *Tyrannobdella rex*

Size: Up to 3 inches (7.6 centimeters) long

Diet: Blood

Habitat: Moist, tropical regions of South America

Predators and threats: Fish, birds, large insects, and snakes will all eat leeches. Snails and mites will also eat leech eggs.

Never judge the GOBLIN SHARK by its teeth.

Few animals are more feared than the shark, and the **GOBLIN SHARK**'s unique face is enough to give you nightmares. But those jaws are useful! When a meal approaches, the shark's jaws thrust forward, then suck up prey like a vacuum. Though it looks scary, the goblin shark is another innocent monster. Since it inhabits such deep waters, it doesn't pose any threat to humans.

Misunderstood Monsters

Do "monstrous" animals get left out when it comes to **conservation**? Research suggests that we are more likely to want to save animal species that are cute and furry. But every animal is important in an **ecosystem**, so it's crucial to protect those that seem ugly or even scary. As **"living fossils,"** goblin sharks can provide us with clues to discover the history of life on Earth!

Name: Goblin shark

Species name: *Mitsukurina owstoni*

Size: Roughly 10–13 feet (3–4 meters) long

Diet: Fish, cephalopods, crustaceans, and isopods

Habitat: It is rare to spot a goblin shark, but their recorded sightings indicate a wide range. They have been seen in the Atlantic Ocean, the Pacific Ocean, the Indian Ocean, and the Gulf of Mexico, and survive in waters up to 4,265 feet (1,300 meters) deep.

Predators and threats: Humans do not intentionally fish for goblin sharks, yet they are sometimes caught in fishing nets by accident. Because goblin sharks usually keep to themselves in deep waters, such accidents are rare.

Chill out with the KOMODO DRAGON.

The **KOMODO DRAGON** is the largest lizard in the world, but this dragon doesn't fly or chase after knights. Instead, it waits. Silent and stealthy, it sits in one spot until a meal walks by, then strikes, releasing toxic proteins as it chews. When its prey has weakened from the injury, the Komodo feasts.

Icky Eaters!

Komodo dragons aren't picky eaters, and they will take every opportunity to score a meal—even if it means eating their own species. The greatest danger to Komodo dragons is other dragons, especially hungry adults. Komodo dragons also raid the graves of local villages. To deter the dragons from digging up corpses, villagers often pile rocks on their gravesites.

Name: Komodo dragon

Species name: *Varanus komodoensis*

Size: Roughly 8.5 feet long (2.6 meters), including the tail. The largest specimen found was 10.3 feet (3.1 meters) long.

Diet: Meat! Deer, boar, goats, water buffalo, and carrion are all Komodo chow.

Habitat: The tropical savanna forests of a few Indonesian islands, including Komodo, Rinca, Padar, and Flores

Predators and threats: Komodo dragons have been hunted illegally in the past and are sometimes poisoned by humans to protect livestock. They are listed as vulnerable, although few animals will attempt to hunt Komodos, due to their size. Komodo dragon eggs and young are often preyed upon by adult Komodos.

Back away from the JAPANESE GIANT HORNET.

The **JAPANESE GIANT HORNET** can fly at speeds of over thirty miles an hour, and when it finds a meal (like a tasty honeybee colony), it sends out a **pheromone** signal. This chemical alarm alerts other hornets, telling them to join in the fight. Not scared yet? Each hornet can kill up to forty bees *per minute.*

Honeybees at War

Although honeybees are up against Japanese giant hornets five times their size, they have evolved a defense against them. When a hornet finds a honeybee nest, the honeybees wait until it comes inside. Then they swarm the hornet intruder and begin to vibrate. This vibrating causes the group to heat up and literally *cook* the hornet alive, killing it before it can send out its alarm.

Name: Japanese giant hornet

Species name: *Vespa mandarinia japonica*

Size: 1.8 inches (4.6 centimeters) long

Diet: Insects, such as honeybees. Hornet larvae also secrete a clear fluid that is eaten by the adults and provides an energy boost.

Habitat: The large and small islands of Japan, including Hokkaido, Honshu, Shikoku, and Kyushu. They are found in high-altitude forests of tropical and temperate areas, typically using hollow trees as nests.

Predators and threats: Humans are the biggest threat to Japanese giant hornets, and in some Japanese mountain villages, these creatures are considered a delicacy. But the tables often turn, and thirty to forty people die every year in Japan from giant hornet stings.

Look out for the HUMBOLDT SQUID.

What has three hearts, a razor-sharp beak, and weighs up to one hundred pounds? Meet the **HUMBOLDT SQUID**, one of the most intelligent predators in the water. Also known as *diablo rojo* (Spanish for "red devil"), Humboldt squid hunt together in **shoals** of up to 1,200 individuals and use "flash talk" to communicate—changing color quickly from red to white. What are they saying to each other? Nobody knows—yet.

Release the Kraken!

The kraken, a legendary Scandinavian sea monster, is said to be inspired by sightings of the giant squid (close cousin of the Humboldt). The kraken is often depicted with its tentacles wrapped around a ship, dragging sailors to their watery graves. In real life, giant squid don't attack ships, but they have been known to attack full-grown, fifty-foot-long sperm whales.

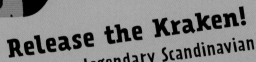

Name: Humboldt squid

Species name: *Dosidicus gigas*

Size: Mantle up to roughly 6 feet (1.8 meters) long, reaching 8.2 feet (2.5 meters), including tentacles

Diet: Shrimp, mollusks, lanternfish, and other cephalopods. Humboldt squid are also known to eat their own kind that have been hurt or captured in fishing nets.

Habitat: The deep waters of the eastern Pacific, from Tierra del Fuego to California. They have also been spotted as far north as Sitka, Alaska.

Predators and threats: Sharks, sperm whales, seals, swordfish, and marlin all feed on adult Humboldt squid. As juveniles, large fish and gulls are common predators.

Wave hello to the HUMAN!

Why are humans in a book about monsters? We aren't born with sharp fangs, venom, or even **camouflage** to keep us hidden. But we do have one thing that makes us formidable foes—big brains. Our intelligence has allowed us to survive on every continent on the planet by developing tools to fend off predators and technology to improve our chances for survival. But this comes at a price. Pollution from industry and cars, habitat destruction, overfishing, and overhunting are all consequences of human development.

Wise Weapons

Humans have a long history of using our big brains to create weapons to help us survive. Historians believe that spears were created in 400,000 BC, with **atlatls**, boomerangs, and arrowheads following soon after. Humans also use other species as weapons, such as police dogs that are specially trained to guard officers and subdue enemies. Metal weapons, gunpowder, rockets, submarines, guns, bombs, and missiles are all human creations.

Name: Human

Species name: *Homo sapiens*

Size: Human sizes vary greatly. The tallest recorded human was 8 feet 11.1 inches (2.7 meters), while the shortest was 1 foot 9.5 inches (54.6 centimeters). The global average is just below 5 feet 6 inches (167.6 centimeters).

Diet: Humans are omnivores, capable of eating both plants and animals. Human diets vary by region.

Habitat: Humans have learned to survive all over the world, in groups ranging from isolated villages to large cities.

Predators and threats: Modern medicine and technology allow humans to avoid diseases and outwit most predators, yet they are still vulnerable to certain ailments, such as malaria, HIV/AIDS, cancer, and heart disease. Some creatures, such as venomous snakes, hippopotamuses, tigers, and crocodiles, may attack and kill humans. Humans have also been known to kill their own kind, often in great numbers.

All of these creatures have adapted incredible ways of surviving.
Are they cruel or clever? Cute or cunning?
What makes a monster?
You decide.

Inspired by Nature: What traits do famous monsters share with these animals?
Can you think of other monstrous pairs?

Dracula—vampire bat

Zombies—cordyceps fungus

Kraken—giant squid

The Blob—tyrant leech king

Godzilla—Komodo dragon

Frankenstein—assassin bug

Is it a monster? Look closely!

Are you afraid of certain animals? Have you thought about why? All of the animals in this book are terrifying in some ways, but they are all trying to survive using the tools they have.

When you come across scary creatures, ask yourself:

1. Why do I think this animal is scary? Is it because of how it looks? Does it behave monstrously?

2. Does the scary trait help the animal survive in some way?

3. Are there any similarities between myself and the animal I'm afraid of?

Once you've answered these questions, you might not see them as monsters at all!

Say What?! A Glossary of Useful Words

Some of the words in the text are in **bold.** If you didn't understand them,
you can use the list below to learn the definition for new terms.

- **Adaptation:** the process of change by which an organism becomes more suited to its environment
- **Amphibian:** a group of cold-blooded animals that have gills and live in water as larvae, but breathe air as adults
- **Atlatl:** (pronounced "aht-LAHT-ul") a stick with a hook on one end and a handle on the other, used for throwing a spear or a dart
- **Biodiversity:** the number of different species of plants and animals in an environment
- **Bloodletting:** a medical practice that involves withdrawing blood from a patient to treat or prevent diseases
- **Brood parasite:** an animal that manipulates other animal species into caring for its young
- **Bubonic plague:** a very serious disease, caused by the bacterium *Yersinia pestis,* resulting in fever, headache, chills, and possibly death
- **Camouflage:** hiding from predators, often by blending in with the surroundings
- **Circulation:** the movement of blood through the body, caused by pumping of the heart
- **Colony:** a group of the same animals living in one place
- **Conservation:** the act of preserving or protecting wildlife or the natural environment
- **Ecosystem:** a community of organisms functioning as a unit with their environment
- **Exoskeleton:** the hard body covering of some invertebrate animals, particularly arthropods
- **Infanticide:** the act of intentionally causing the death of an infant animal
- **Keratin:** a protein that is found in numerous animals, forming hair, nails, hooves, feathers, and claws
- **Living fossil:** an organism related to a long-extinct family, known only from fossils
- **Nematocyst:** a specialized cell found in the tentacles of some creatures, containing a venomous coiled barb that can be discharged in self-defense
- **Parasite:** an organism that lives in or on another organism (called its host), obtaining nourishment at the expense of its host
- **Pharyngeal jaws:** a second set of jaws, contained within an animal's throat
- **Pheromone:** a chemical produced by an animal, released into the environment, that influences the behavior or bodily processes of other animals of the same species
- **Pincer:** the front claw of an arthropod, used for carrying loads, defense against others, or attacking prey

- **Regurgitate:** to bring swallowed food back up into the mouth
- **Shoal:** a large number of fish that swims together for social reasons (they become a "school" when they swim together in a coordinated direction!)
- **Spores:** tiny, single-celled reproductive units, produced by non-flowering plants, fungi, and algae
- **Tumor cell:** a cancerous cell that grows at a fast pace
- **Zooids:** (pronounced "ZOH-oidz") the distinct individuals that form a larger animal

THIS IS A BORZOI BOOK PUBLISHED BY ALFRED A. KNOPF   Text copyright © 2017 by Jess Keating   Jacket art and interior illustrations copyright © 2017 by David DeGrand
All rights reserved. Published in the United States by Alfred A. Knopf, an imprint of Random House Children's Books, a division of Penguin Random House LLC, New York.
Knopf, Borzoi Books, and the colophon are registered trademarks of Penguin Random House LLC.

Visit us on the Web! randomhousekids.com   Educators and librarians, for a variety of teaching tools, visit us at RHTeachersLibrarians.com

Library of Congress Cataloging-in-Publication Data
Names: Keating, Jess, author. | DeGrand, David, illustrator.   Title: What makes a monster? : discovering the world's scariest creatures / by Jess Keating ; with illustrations by David DeGrand.
Description: "An informative introduction to nature's scariest creatures, exploring why some animals are considered 'monsters.'" —Provided by publisher
New York : Alfred A. Knopf, [2017] | Audience: Ages 7–10.   Identifiers: LCCN 2016029356 (print) | LCCN 2016032299 (ebook) |
ISBN 978-0-553-51230-4 (trade) | ISBN 978-0-553-51231-1 (lib. bdg.) | ISBN 978-0-553-51232-8 (ebook)
Subjects: LCSH: Animals—Miscellanea—Juvenile literature. | Dangerous animals—Juvenile literature. | Animals—Folklore—Juvenile literature.
Classification: LCC QL49 .K35 2017 (print) | LCC QL49 (ebook) | DDC 591.6—dc23

The illustrations in this book were created using ink and digital coloring.
MANUFACTURED IN CHINA   August 2017   10 9 8 7 6 5 4 3 2 1   First Edition
Random House Children's Books supports the First Amendment and celebrates the right to read.